at Westminster Pier for the boat journey
DLR to Tower Gateway.

HOW TO REACH THE START:
Bank Station, with its DLR platform, is part of the London
Underground network, reached by the Circle and District Line (at
Monument Station), Waterloo & City, the Northern Line and Central
Line. To reach Tower Gateway Station on the DLR, exit from Tower
Hill Station (District and Circle Lines), face the Tower of London,
turn left, pass by the Roman wall, take the underpass in front of
you and then the escalator.

THE BEST SEATS:
When taking the DLR, try to sit in the front of the train or facing for-
ward for the best view. And there will be more items of interest to
be seen if you sit on the right hand side of the train leaving from
Bank or Tower Gateway, or the left hand side when setting out from
Island Gardens.
     Take a DLR train to Island Gardens, and get off at Canary
Wharf if stopping there.

WE'RE OFF:
When either emerging into the light from the Bank tunnel, or setting
off from Tower Gateway, we start right away to locate the points of
interest and their history. Some of these sights will appear and dis-
appear fairly quickly, so to have read this booklet before setting out,
or before the return journey, will be to your advantage.

1 When standing a little way down the platform at Tower Gateway
Station, Cesar Pelli's **Canary Wharf Tower** can be seen in the distance. You will see it again several times.
     Almost as soon as you set off from **Tower Gateway** Station,
look back to the right, directly after the multi-storey car park, for a
quick glimpse of **Tower Bridge** and the **Tower of London**.
     You may well have visited them already because of their fame.

Suffice it to say that the Tower probably has Roman origins, but the central fortification, of Keep or White Tower, was built around 1078. Both prison and royal residence in its time, the Tower of London houses the Crown Jewels and has a motley and sometimes bloody history.

Tower Bridge is modern by comparison, it being a Victorian construction (1894).

2 The large, white stone and glass building seen beyond rooftops to the right is **Thomas More Square**, a complex of offices and a Safeway supermarket. (Sir Thomas More, the famous English Chancellor, lawyer, wit, scholar and lover of the arts, was found guilty of perjury by King Henry VIII's Parliament. He was executed in 1535 and had his head "fixed upon London Bridge".)

St. Katharine Dock, next to it but out of view, was opened in 1828 with the firing of cannon and with several decorated sailing ships entering the new dock from the River Thames. The dock was only moderately successful, trading in ivory, scent, shells, wool and indigo. Now, however, it is well worth a visit (very close to the Tower of London) to see its yachts, original Ivory House, shops, eating places and the Dickens Inn.

3 Beyond the buildings to the right, between you and the Thames, was the now mostly filled-in **London Dock**. This was a complex of several docks, built in the early 1800s. A great success as docks with vast storage warehouses for everything from wool, rubber, wine, spirits, spices, tobacco, etc., it was not until the advent of containers, large ships and expensive labour that they became uneconomical to operate. Most of the site was levelled and the docks filled in. Now only Shadwell Basin, Hermitage Basin and some ornamental connecting strips of water remain.

Bank Station

Tower Gateway

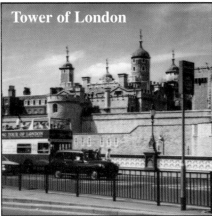

Tower of London

Tower Bridge

St. George-in-the-East

DLR and St. Anne's

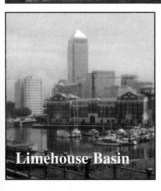

Limehouse Basin

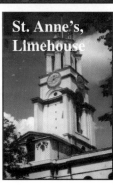

St. Anne's, Limehouse

The Old Sugar Warehouse

4 Appearing several times on the right hand side, when seen above and between buildings, and after three tower blocks, is the white tower and four domed turrets of **St. George-in-the-East** church. Its imposing stone structure has stood since 1729. Designed by Nicholas Hawksmoor (a pupil of Wren and Vanbrugh), it was one of 13 proposed churches ordered by Queen Anne to commemorate Marlborough's victories on the continent. Captain Bligh of (mutiny on) the Bounty worshipped there with his family. Gutted in the war, a new and smaller church has been cleverly built inside. After it you may then catch a glimpse of the spire of **St. Paul's, Shadwell.**

5 You have now reached **SHADWELL** Station. Beyond a stone Victorian church and spire on the right hand side, and looking slightly backwards, is the elegant spire of **St. Paul's, Shadwell**. Standing right next to Shadwell Basin (part of the already men-tioned London Dock), the church has a maritime history, with many sea captains buried in the churchyard. Although what you see was constructed in 1820, the crypt was of a much earlier date (1656). Captain Cook was a parishioner. His son was baptised there, as was Jane Randolph, Thomas Jefferson's mother. (Thomas Jefferson, 1743-1826, was the third president of the United States of America.)

The name Shadwell comes from its sweet water wells that were once famous for their curative properties.

6 Still looking to the right hand side, after a greenish coloured block of flats, you will see in the middle distance the tops of a red brick, slab-sided and angular building. It is **Free Trade Wharf**. Part of the 1870 wharfage and warehouses remain beside the modern block of up-market riverside flats.

The name "Free Trade" may have originated when duties were substantially lowered in the 18th century, or possibly when the wharf was given for trade, free of duty, to Dutch sea traders who supplied London with food and fuel during the Great Plague of 1664-1665.

7 **Do not dwell on the left hand side for your first DLR journey. There is more to see on the right**. But over to the left and deep into the distance for this whole stretch from Tower Gateway/Bank to almost Canary Wharf is London's **East End**.

Sociologists and historians are fascinated by the East End, an enormous area of London which has been such a separate part of it. Spreading rapidly and with no overall plan during the Industrial Revolution, it had no civic focal point. And so, with no hotels or restaurants to speak of, there was little to attract outsiders to the area. It was also isolated by being kept at arm's length by the merchants of the City, who used it as an industrial and dockland area. The modern developments in Docklands have helped to rejuvenate the area, as has the great improvement in public transport, like the DLR and Jubilee Line Extension.

For those interested in domestic architecture there is a feast for the eyes to be had when looking out of the left hand side. There is 18th century elegance (including a 1724 church), Victorian artisan and impoverished dwellings, Edwardian size, '20s and '30s utility blocks (some brought up to date recently), other rejuvenated buildings and modern estates.

8 Directly ahead, as you enter and leave **LIMEHOUSE** Station, you will see the white tower of **St. Anne's, Limehouse** church (more on it later). When you are at the station and as soon as the train leaves, look down to the right to see **Limehouse Basin** with its yachts at their moorings. The dock's curved shape accommodates the Limehouse Link road tunnel, an artery between Central London, Canary Wharf, London City Airport and the east of England north of the Thames.

Limehouse Basin was formerly Regent's Canal Dock, handling mainly general cargo, timber and coal. You will see, almost beneath the train, where the Regent's Canal joins the Basin.

Also from here, ahead and to the right, is a good view of **Canary Wharf**, with its high tower as a focal point.

9 Immediately to the left of the train you might catch a glimpse of the continuation of **Regent's Canal** and a lock. Most of the business of Regent's Canal Dock was to off-load cargo into barges for waterborne transport north throughout England on the Regent's Canal and then the Grand Union Canal. Little used, the Regent's Canal is now a tranquil stretch of water, much favoured by fishermen.

Like many such sleepy canals now in the UK, they were, before the general use of railways and roads, once busy and vital arteries for transporting bulky and heavy goods throughout the kingdom.

A mile or so along the waterway's bank, and housed in canal-side warehouses, is the **Ragged School Museum**, at 46-48 Copperfield Road. To commemorate Dr. Barnado, who provided homes, food and education for destitute children of the East End, it houses the simple artefacts of everyday life - mostly Victorian - and is much enjoyed by children.

Look back quickly to Limehouse Basin again. Close to where Narrow Street crosses the Basin entrance via a swing bridge is Horseferry Road. Here dockers were once "called off the stones" for employment. When the foreman threw work "tallies" into the air, there would be an animal scramble and fight for the opportunity to gain a day's wage.

10 On the far left hand side as you look at Limehouse Basin, another canal (**Limehouse Cut**) snakes its way beneath the railway line and away to the left hand side. This 1770 waterway was dug across the oxbow of the Isle of Dogs to save barge traffic on the river Lea (or Lee) from having to navigate the dangerous tidal waters past Blackwall and Greenwich.

Then glance to the right to see a brick building, with balconies seemingly held to spiky rods (see No.13).

Canary Wharf

Station arches

Cabot Place East

Mackenzie Walk

Cabot Square

Lunch break

Looking south

One Canada Square

West India Quay

11 You may have seen it already ahead of you when at Limehouse Station, but look to the left now to see the massive white stone tower of **St. Anne's, Limehouse** (1724), surmounted by a mast, golden ball and weather vane. This is another Hawksmoor church with a clock, thought to be the highest church clock in England. The church tower served as a navigational landmark for those on the river, and the clock as a means for sailors to check their timepieces. You will be closest to it as the train passes beneath a series of metal arches.

12 On either side is historic **Limehouse,** once the district of London's Chinese community, with its then narrow and seedy streets. This Chinatown of the past was a place of opium dens and the haunt of gamblers and prostitutes. Charles Dickens drew inspiration from the area, describing it in "Great Expectations", "Our Mutual Friend", "Dombey and Son" and "The Uncommercial Traveller".

The Chinese community have now made Gerrard Street and its surroundings in London's West End their new Chinatown.

The name Limehouse may be derived from "lime oasts" - oasts being another word for kilns.

13 You have now reached **WESTFERRY** Station and, soon after it, there is a fine and much closer view ahead of the **Canary Wharf** complex of large buildings, with Cesar Pelli's beautifully proportioned tower rising above them (details of Canary Wharf and what to see there comes later in this guide).

On the right hand side of the train, and looking back a little, is a tall, yellow brick building with spikes protruding from the top and suspended balconies. This is **Dundee Wharf**, which stands beside **Limekiln Creek**. Here, from medieval days, stood lime kilns, fed chalk and fuel by sailing ships and barges moored at Limekiln Dock.

Looking down from the train to the left is West India Dock Road, once famous for the insalubrious Charlie Brown's pub.

Decorated profusely with artefacts from around the world, it was the haunt of lascars, other sailors and, of course, ladies of ill repute.

14 We have now reached the **West India Docks**, and down to the right, as the train climbs slowly upward, is the entrance to the Import Dock, once having a stone gateway surmounted by a bronze sailing ship. Close by is the Dockmaster's House, now a restaurant, and a huge and magnificent sugar warehouse (1802), to be converted.

West India Docks, established in the marshy waste land of the Isle of Dogs, was built by the West India Company and started in 1800 to protect the company's goods from land based and river-borne thieves. This was the first wall-protected dock. And so successful was it that other walled docks were soon to follow. Produce dealt with at its wharves and in the warehouses were mainly sugar and rum, but also molasses, coffee, cotton, cocoa, ginger and pimento.

15 The train climbs and then turns sharply to the right into **WEST INDIA QUAY** Station. Look left toward Poplar (named for the trees grown as windbreaks for shipping) to see a yellow and red brick building with a suspended roof. This is the new **Billingsgate Fish Market,** taking over from the original one close to the Tower of London where once fishing boats delivered their catch for sale. Beyond it, and within a bend of the river, is the site of the **National Millennium Exhibition**.

Down to the right, over dock water, is a pedestrian bridge that connects Canary Wharf's Cabot Square with West India Quay and the old sugar warehouse.

16 On January the 11th, 1660, **Samuel Pepys**, before he attained high office, walked across the Isle of Dogs below where West India Quay Station now stands. He had reached Blackwall by barge on a cold day to be present at the launching of a man-of-war, the Royal

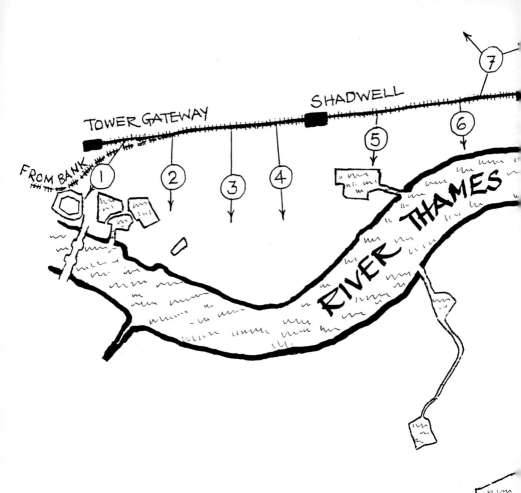

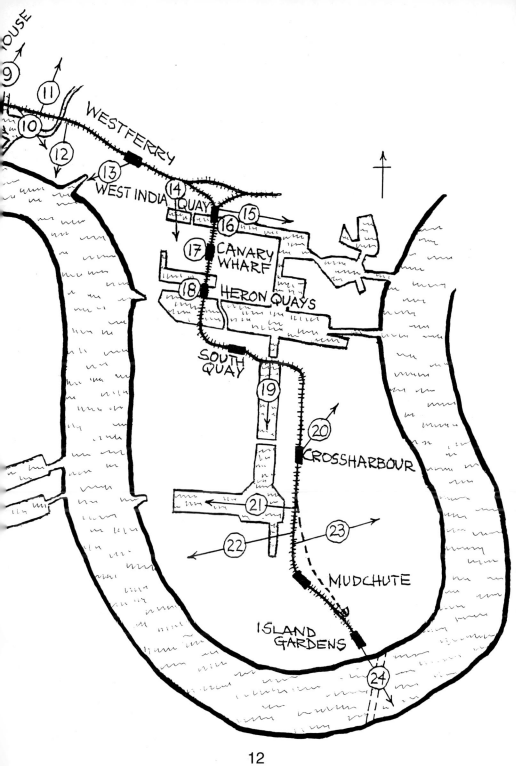

9 → TOUSE

11

10

WESTFERRY

12

13

WEST INDIA QUAY 14

15

16

17 CANARY WHARF

18 HERON QUAYS

SOUTH QUAY

19

20 CROSSHARBOUR

21

22

23

MUDCHUTE

ISLAND GARDENS

24

Oake. He then decided to fortify himself with burnt wine at the taverns there and to walk back to London, via Limehouse, to check the ropemakers' output and potential capacity in Ropemakers' Fields (the street is there in Limehouse). In the days of sail it was essential, especially in time of conflict, that there would be an ample supply of rope for the Navy's sailing ships.

Ahead lies the arch and glass covered **CANARY WHARF** Station, where you may care to get off (on the left hand side of the train) to wander around.

17 You have now reached **CANARY WHARF** Station - Canary Wharf being so named because it was formerly a dock that handled bananas from the Canary Islands.

CANARY WHARF

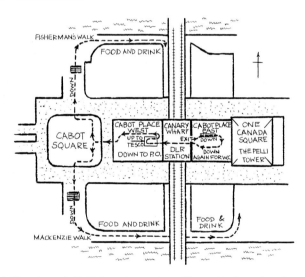

If you would like to visit this almost self-contained mini-city, alight from the left hand side of the train. There you will see a main entrance to **Canary Wharf**. Go through it and you will find yourself on the first floor beneath a large glass dome. This is **Cabot Place East.** (John Cabot, 1450-1498, was an Italian navigator and explorer of North America.). On the floor above are eating places. Below and around you are shops that you may care to visit. In front is Books etc.

Take the escalator down to the ground floor. In front of you is the entrance to **One Canada Square** - the Cesar Pelli tower. It has 50 floors, is 800' (244 metres) tall, and is designed to sway 13 3/4" in the strongest winds. As the tower houses offices only, there is no entry for tourists, except on special occasions.

The public lavatories are off the Concourse on the floor below.

Turn around, look at the shops, and walk through doors to beneath the DLR station and over a compass rose. Pass through another set of doors into **Cabot Place West**, **Cabot Hall** where, directly in front of you, is the **Tourist Information Centre**. Here you may obtain free leaflets, excellent guides and books on Docklands (such as mine), information on the shops, pubs, cafés and restaurants at Canary Wharf, and tickets for events in Docklands and elsewhere in London.

To the side of the Information Centre is an escalator down to the **Concourse**. Here there are shops, Banks, cash dispensers, and a **Post Office**. Already you will have seen that most things you may desire are obtainable within the Canary Wharf complex. There are shops, cafés and pubs all around.

Just behind the Tourist Information Centre on the ground floor are escalators to the **Tesco Metro** supermarket above. Above that again is **Gallery West.**

Still on the ground floor, pass or visit the cafés and shops, take the doors ahead and cross the road to **Cabot Square**. This is the place for sitting out by the fountain and waterfalls in summertime to watch the world go by.

You could now either return to the DLR, retracing your path, or take steps down to the waterside on either side to visit the excellent dockside restaurants, bars, pubs and cafés on your way back to Canary Wharf Station.

Cascades

Contraband Chimney

The George Pub

South Quay Footbridge

The best view

London Arena

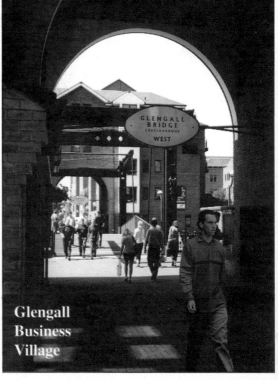

Glengall Business Village

18 HERON QUAYS Station comes immediately after Canary Wharf. To the left is the new **Canary Wharf Station** for the Jubilee Line Extension - part of the London Underground network. On the right you will see the sloping **Cascades** building with its nautical motifs. Then, abutting the dock water, is Britannia Hotels, **The International**.

As you leave Heron Quays Station, look down to the left to see the impressive, serpentine shaped, angled column and cable pedestrian bridge connecting Canary Wharf to South Quay.

The train will soon turn sharply to the left to **SOUTH QUAY** Station. With buildings of modern design on its left hand side, the station is notorious for the IRA bomb that was detonated beneath it causing much devastation on the 9th of February, 1996.

19 Soon after leaving **South Quay** Station, and immediately after the train turns a little to the right and then left, look to the right, down **Millwall Inner Dock** (1868) to **Glengall Bridge**. On the quayside to the left is the slab-sided **London Arena**, and almost beneath you a Thames sailing barge used in the evacuation of troops from Dunkirk. The train will then turn sharply to the right.

20 As the train approaches **CROSSHARBOUR AND LONDON ARENA**, you will see the **London Arena** on the right hand side. This is the venue for conferences, boxing, basketball, concerts and other events. To the left of it are the offices, homes, shops and refreshment places of Pepper Street and **Glengall Business Village**.

Look back and to the left when at the station to note a pub called **The George**. As at Horseferry Road in Limehouse (already mentioned), this was another site for calling dockers "off the stones" for work.

21 Having left **CROSSHARBOUR**, you will see an ASDA super-market to the left, and then, on the right, a solitary brick **chimney**

stack. This was where Customs and Excise burnt contraband when the docks were in operation.

Beyond this chimney stack is **Millwall Outer Dock**, a continuation of Millwall Inner Dock.

These docks were so named when they were constructed in 1865 because there were several windmills on the river wall. Grain became the dock's main commodity, and flour milling one of its industries.

On a ghoulish note, it was on the nearby river bank of the Isle of Dogs that tarred bodies of malefactors were suspended from **gibbets** to deter sailors approaching London by water from causing mischief.

On a lighter note, it was from this dock that graceful Swedish ships, like Britannia, once sailed with cargo and passengers to Stockholm. The vessels were staffed by notoriously attractive stewardesses.

22 Over to the right, on the river bank beyond domestic housing, an enormous ship (about 700' or 213 metres long) was conceived and built by I. K. Brunel in 1851. (Isambard Kingdom Brunel, 1806-1859, was an English engineer of extraordinary diversity, building railways, bridges, tunnels, docks, piers, buildings, guns and ships.) The **Great Eastern** was powered by sail, paddle wheels and a screw. She was launched broadside on because of the narrowness of the river at that point, but got stuck on the slipway for three months - causing the company that built her to go bankrupt. An immensely strong, innovative, but costly failure, she somewhat redeemed herself toward the end of her life by laying the first Atlantic cable in 1866.

23 Over to the left among the greenery is **Mudchute City Farm**, where children can mingle with farm animals. The rough contours of the ground were created by spoil from the excavations of the Millwall Dock over the years 1865-1868.

And almost beneath you, on the left hand side in Millwall Park, see the construction of a tunnel beneath the Thames for the DLR to reach Greenwich and Lewisham by the year 2000.

24 From **MUDCHUTE** Station you approach **ISLAND GARDENS** Station. Look ahead to the right and left to catch a glimpse of the masts and rigging of the **Cutty Sark** clipper ship (see later section on Greenwich) and the cupolas of Sir Christopher Wren's **Royal Naval College** that he designed as a trial for the dome of St. Paul's (again, see later section on Greenwich). Beyond them, and a bit to the right, on the hill in Greenwich Park, is the **Old Royal Observatory** and the **Timeball** (see APPROACH TO GREEN-WICH).

APPROACH TO GREENWICH

After alighting from the DLR (there's a public convenience across the road that runs beneath the station) carry on toward the river and the brick and glass-domed rotunda where the lift or stairs will take you down to the **Greenwich Foot Tunnel** (fondly known as **"the pipe"**, and not to be missed). But before you do so, pass through the gateway to the gardens on the left to admire a wonder-ful view of Wren's **Royal Naval College**, the **Cutty Sark** and, on the hill beyond in delightful Greenwich Park, the **Old Royal Observatory**.

Notice the red **Timeball** on a mast at the Observatory. With luck you may be within sight of it at around 1300 hours. The ball was designed when the river was full of sailing ships and accurate time essential for navigation at sea. Navigators would correct their chronometers by watching this ball with eye or through telescope from the river Thames. Since 1833 the ball has been wound up the mast and allowed to fall at exactly 1300 hours each day (at 1 o'clock because astronomers were always busy at 12 o'clock mea-suring the sun).

The **Tunnel** (narrow to start with because a German bomb fell

Greenwich
Foot
Tunnel

Tunnel Rotunda

Greenwich

Cutty Sark

Cutty Sark

The
Yacht
Pub

The Trafalgar Pub

Royal Naval College and Queen's House

Greenwich Park

Cutty
Sark
Pub

The Timeball

nearby in the war and it had to be reinforced with an iron sleeve) was built in 1902 for dockers to reach their work. It is lined with 200,000 white tiles. Notices warn you not to smoke, spit, cycle, busk, loiter, litter, skate, skateboard or allow your animal to foul. So you have been warned!

GREENWICH

Historic Greenwich is best known for its **Old Royal Observatory** and the **Meridian** (Longitude zero, from which Greenwich Mean Time is measured).

The Observatory was designed by Sir Christopher Wren, at the command of King Charles II, and founded in 1675. The cost was £520 9s 1d, obtained by selling 690 barrels of old gunpowder.

The **Timeball** has been mentioned.

The clipper ship, **Cutty Sark**, is also one of the sights of Greenwich. The vessel was named after a short shirt of Paisley linen, and taken from the Robert Burns poem Tam O'Shanter. Launched in 1869, she sailed the seven seas with cargoes of tea, coal, jute, oil, wool, buffalo horn and scrap iron, etc. Both on and below deck you will get a feel for life on a working ship in the days of sail. There is also a fine collection of ships' figureheads to be seen inside.

Other sights of note in Greenwich are the **Queen's House** (designed by Inigo Jones in 1616), the **National Maritime Museum** and Sir Francis Chichester's **Gipsy Moth IV**.

More information may be obtained from the **Tourist Information Centre** at 46 Greenwich Church Street.

THREE PUBS ON THE RIVER

There are many excellent pubs and places in which to eat in Greenwich. Here I just mention three pubs where you may eat, drink and watch the comings and goings on the river.

Walk along the riverside pathway past Greenwich Pier (where you might later take a boat back to the Tower, Charing Cross or Westminster) and then in front of the **Royal Naval College** (where there is a fine view of the red **Timeball** falling at 1300 hours) to find a Regency pub with bow-fronted windows on the river. This is **The Trafalgar** (famous for its whitebait).

Right behind The Trafalgar, and along a narrow alleyway, is **The Yacht** pub, where you will obtain an excellent view of the river as you eat and drink.

Beyond The Yacht, and past **Trinity Hospital** (1613) (where you might sit on a bench outside among the roses in summertime to view the river and possibly eat a sandwich), is **The Cutty Sark**, a Georgian pub with 17th century origins. Sit outside by the river wall, or in the spacious upstairs room where bow-fronted windows allow you to have a fine view of the Thames and Isle of Dogs.

THE RETURN JOURNEY

You may decide to return to The Tower, Charing Cross or Westminster by river, remembering that your all-day bus and Underground pass will not cover the cost of it. Or you might like to return by "the pipe" and the DLR. When on your way back, or starting from Island Gardens, refer to my map with its numbered arrows. These show you in which direction to look for points of interest. The directions will now be reversed.

I hope that this guide will give much added pleasure to your journey of discovery through such a vibrant part of London.